TIPS

By
MEL JOHNSON

MOODY PRESS

CHICAGO

Contents

23228

Preface

THE OVERWHELMING MAJORITY of you teens are history makers with searching eyes. You want to be strong enough to challenge, but you are still polite enough to be challenged. You ask questions, but you have the courage to listen to honest answers. That makes you good investments.

The information, inspiration, and counsel offered in this book may sound like things you've heard before from parents, pastors, teachers, peers, and others who care. I pledge to tell it like it is, to the point with a positive note. Then, without laboring the point, I'll leave the rest to your intelligence.

The final chapters in this book are written especially for the over-thirty-five generation that wants to understand you, get along with you, and learn to meet your needs. But don't stop reading. Much of it is what you've told me about yourselves and wanted me to tell the unaware and the uninformed.

Tips for Teens is designed to enliven you and those in your life with action and reaction. But more importantly, understanding, sincerity, and respect are stressed. Let's concentrate on closing the gap—not between generations but between people.

1

Home Is Where the Table Is

HAVE YOU EVER CALLED your parents stupid? I hope not! If you did, I sure hope you apologized. All over town there are scores of twosomes called parents who are smart people with so much love in their hearts for their teenagers that they will never tell on you. Let's face it, they are the only two people in the world who love you in spite of all they know about you.

A mother recently complained, "I've just been called stupid by my seventeen-year-old daughter. I thought her observation was just a localized reaction, but she tells me it's unanimous on Main Street."

Here are a few reasons I've been given for calling parents stupid:

1. They are too old-fashioned and out of touch.

2. They don't understand me.

3. I'm tired of hearing of the good old days when they trudged to school twenty miles every day barefoot in the snow.

4. I'm tired of seeing all their report cards with those high grades. What about the ones they don't show me?

5. I'm tired of hearing, "Based on my experience—"

6. They're too suspicious. They always imagine the worst. They're always giving me the third degree.

Are these real hangups? Sure they are, but they don't make your parents stupid. Let's find out how smart they really are.

"Hey, Mom, this theme is due tomorrow, and I need help on the research."

"Dad, I get my driver's permit tomorrow. Don't forget you have to go with me."

Why should anyone want a stupid person to help with re-

search or an idiot adult to go along to meet the driving examiner?

"Remind me to get the hamburger buns for the picnic, Mom, and oh, would you please bring my clarinet to school? You've got to; I forgot it."

How could a stupid parent remember to do things like that?

"Mom, be sure to have dinner early so Dad can drive me to the game. And I need money." (Money, money—sounds like a broken record.)

How in the wide world can a set of stupid parents take care of all these things? But they will, because that is the kind of stuff they are made of. You get my point, don't you? Your parents are the sole owners and underpaid operators of the "Stupid Parents' Taxi Service." It sure is nice to be needed.

Seriously, all this stuff about their report cards and their being old-fashioned may be true, but your parents are worth more than you will ever be able to pay them. Their love is deep. Their concern is genuine.

Get smart! Appreciate and love those folks early. Get into practice now, so there will be no days of regret in the years ahead.

"Honour thy father and mother . . . that it may be well with thee" (Ephesians 6:2-3).

2

The Shut-Out Club

"WE USED TO BE SO CLOSE, but I don't get through to my parents anymore. It's just one fight after another."

"Our son comes home from school and disappears. Oh, the body's there but he pulls down the curtain."

Sounds like both parents and teenagers here are candidates for the Shut-Out Club. Members of the club talk *at*, not *with* each other.

Are you hurt because the one you love has turned you off? Are problems in your home characterized by the reactions of threatened people? Parents feel threatened because they think their teenagers are resisting authority and want too much too soon. Teens feel threatened because they are told what to do when they want to begin making their own decisions.

When two threatened people get together, it is easy for both to end up screaming. Angry people say things they don't mean. Distraught parents punish too harshly. Privileges disappear; resentment sets in.

How can we mend this communication breakdown before it jams all the family machinery? A one-sided talk that turns out to be a lecture or a heated discussion filled with defensive interruptions won't help matters. You can't fill the generation gap with hot air, but you can bridge it. Learn the art of talking *with* people instead of *at* them. Here are some suggestions to keep you out of the Shut-Out Club:

1. Next time you are about to explode, take a long walk instead. Get inside your parents and try to understand why they act the way they do. Analyze pressures.

2. Turn on with love, listening, and sincerity. I think every-

7

one wants an interested, unflappable ear. Keep in mind that listening doesn't include opinions unless asked. Too often teens can't resist the old, worn-out phrase, "You just don't understand," and parents can't resist nailing a few moral spikes to the platform. Too many of us have bad cases of interruptionitis already.

3. See the good side and say it. That's a four-bit phrase that's packed full of good sense. What a conscientious parent or teen expects of their loved one they usually get, especially if they learn to praise a job well done and set reachable goals for each other.

4. Learn to attack the problem, not each other. A sheepherder in Colorado says that in the presence of coyotes, wild horses put their heads together and proceed to kick their enemy. When the wild donkeys are attacked, they face the enemy and kick each other. Put that together and hang onto it.

5. Have the humility to remember that you may be wrong. Few people are mature enough to admit their mistakes. Only a handful try to find truth in the other person's position. In the all-important world of family relations there are three words almost as powerful as "I love you." They are "maybe you're right."

6. Never let the sun go down on your wrath. Don't let nightfall come without settling your arguments. Keep short accounts with those you love the most. Unfinished fights, unresolved conflicts, and lingering resentments are destructive.

Now you're in conference together and you're talking with each other. I would be foolish to think there were not some domestic fights on the scene. But I don't like to use the word *fight* because it really sounds so brutal. As you talk with each other, just keep in mind that the goal of each battle should not be victory but reconciliation. The goal of each conference should be understanding honesty.

A conference where the participants talk *with* each other rather than *at* each other should end with more respect for the persons involved.

3

Squares in the Family Circle

THERE ARE TIMES when as a growing teenager you want to be heard. Expressing an opinion is like putting mustard and ketchup and pickle on a hot dog—really necessary. But all of a sudden when Mom and Dad are asking questions, or when you know there's something you should tell them, if you're like a lot of teenagers, you close up your conversation piece in a tight-lipped seal. The time they want to know something is just when you don't feel like talking.

Keeping your parents informed will not only help you, but make life a lot richer for them. You'd be surprised what satisfaction and joy you give them when you level with them.

You're the headline story in their lives; and if you cooperate, you'll both mean more to each other.

Angle-players, corner-cutters, sharpshooters, and goof-offs are misfits in the family circle. Here are ten tips to help every teenager get along famously at home.

1. Be obedient. You've heard this before, but it bears repeating because the Bible commands it. "Children, obey your parents in the Lord, for this is right" (Ephesians 6:1).

2. Be respectful. Never be caught referring to Dad and Mom as "the old lady" or "the old man." You'll regret the difficulties you get into for showing such disgraceful disrespect for your parents.

3. Be polite. A refreshing impression is made on people, regardless of their faith, when they meet and hear a teenager who has learned the art of courtesy. You will be a welcome person when from your lips are heard such phrases as "Pardon me," "Thank you," and many other polite and gracious remarks.

4. Remember that your parents are people. Home is not just

a place to eat and sleep. Your parents have your interest at heart; and even though it is sometimes hard for you to accept, you will find that what they want is the very best for their young people. They are zealous for you and are anxious for you to make a success of your life. Don't give them the old brush-off. Don't put on a bored expression when Dad and Mom are talking to you. Pay attention! It pays off.

5. Be ambitious. "Get up and go" is often the key that unlocks Dad's heart (and pocketbook). Today, too many of us seem to feel that we've got a lot coming, and we just sit back and grin, expecting the world to give us whatever we want. Don't get angry at Mom and Dad when you discover that things just don't work out that way. Show some real spunk and find out that energy, enthusiasm, and success are triplets.

6. Don't be blindly led by the group. Don't be afraid to be different. It's really depressing to see teenagers who are afraid the group will laugh at them for the time they spend reading or developing their brains. Why not try the art of being a real individualist without being a hermit? You know what you believe, and you know what you stand for. You will find that even unsaved parents will respect determination to stand fast, even though you may have to do it alone.

7. Don't make demands of your parents. Mother has had a big day, and things just haven't gone the way they should have gone. Dad comes home from a job which has had tensions, conflicts, and insecurities. If you fire complaints, questions, and demands at them as soon as you walk in the door, you cannot really expect a favorable reaction. Why not just wait and sit down as a family and give in detail your opinions on the things that lie on your heart? Family conferences are very good. Try them!

8. Be honest. A phony will soon be found out. Don't hide your feelings and don't sulk behind closed doors when there's something you want to get off your chest. Parents take a great deal of pride in their teenage sons and daughters who have the reputation of being aboveboard and prove it in the home.

11

9. Be careful about careless casualness. It is too often true that a teenager is guilty of the philosophy and attitude of "so what?" It can kill a person's appetite to watch the manners of some teenagers at the dinner table. It could boil your blood to hear their flippant, matter-of-fact language. Your manners must be acceptable in public and in private. Learn to be ladies and gentlemen. Stand up straight to the advice of parents who are more than your friends—they are veterans on the team that wins.

10. Your parents expect consideration. Don't take time for granted. You always gain points when you walk through the front door a few minutes before curfew deadline. One of the signs of maturity is consideration, and one of the best ways to show it is to try your best not to give them cause to worry. If you're going to be a few minutes late, invest a dime in a telephone call.

Your parents read a lot about teenagers getting into trouble, so they're concerned about where you'll be and how these places will influence you.

They want to know where you're going, not only for dates, but for any activities which take you away from the home base.

Your parents aren't really as interested in your heartbeat's curly hair or your girlfriend's terrific wardrobe quite as much as they're concerned about his or her reputation. They want to know what she's like in school and whether or not he's a careful driver. Give them enough facts about your date to let them know that this one will be okay. Parents naturally worry if they don't know what the person you're with is like.

Your parents live a life of their own. When your big night is coming up, give them advance notice so they can fit their schedule to yours. Don't make last-minute demands on their time. In most cases, they'll be willing to make adjustments if you share your plans with them.

Teens who remember these tips are citizens of a home where their parents are happy and healthy for a long, long time.

4

Mind Your Manners

BEWARE! Piercing eyes are following you in school, in church, on the street, in the restaurant—yes, everywhere! People watch what you do, where you go, how you look, what you say, and how you say it. Some people will show this special attention because they want to learn something, but others do it because they want to find fault. Don't rebel because you're in the spotlight. Teenagers were given special attention even from Shakespeare. In one of his plays, he described young life as the "salad days" when you are green in judgment!

Good manners will smooth your way. They are not just a bag of tricks to help you make a good impression or a list of complicated rules that are hard to follow. The basis for all good manners is simply consideration for other people. A selfish, self-centered person concerned only with making a good impression almost surely has bad manners. The following suggestions can add real sparkle to your manners:

1. Be considerate of others by being cheerful. Make it a habit not to wear your troubles on your face.

2. Be considerate of others by keeping your promises in small as well as large matters. Selfish people can always make excuses for not keeping their word.

3. Be considerate of others by being genuinely friendly. Cliques selfishly exclude people and hurt them unnecessarily.

Now that you've tucked that under your hat, let's go on to places and people in regard to manners and courtesy.

Let's start at home. Good manners are not something that you can put on at will, so if you want to feel at ease when you go out for dinner, practice pleasing table manners at home.

Fellows, help your mom or sister to be seated at dinner. You will soon learn to perform this courtesy with ease and pleasure when out on a date. When you leave the table, ask to be excused.

Your church manners tell what kind of an attitude you have toward God, whether you love Him or resent Him, or worse still, just ignore Him as unworthy of your interest. Irreverence is a bad admission that we have no respect for God. Your attitude and conduct in church often tell what kind of home training you have had and reflect your self-respect or lack of it. Gum chewing, whispering to your neighbor, writing notes, giggling, hair combing, and reading Sunday school papers are poor church manners in anyone's book. Stand up straight when the congregation stands to sing a song or pray. Then listen to the minister without slouching down as if you need a bed in your pew. Only tiny children need to nap during church or need to be entertained during the sermon.

We would need a book to cover manners and courtesy on dates. But, if you're a guy, mark these down. A girl will know she's dating a gentleman if he helps her with her coat, opens doors for her, takes her to her door even if the crowd is waiting in the car, makes pleasant conversation, and helps her out of a car or bus.

Of course, there are items of courtesy that a girl should observe, too. Be appreciative of whatever he does for you. Introduce him to your parents and fill him in on your curfew. Don't try to impress him. Just be yourself. And don't be a gold digger; remember, he's on an allowance, too.

Consideration of others is not just for your date and your friends. Consider other patrons in public places. Don't be a loudmouth or a show-off. Be considerate of the waiter or waitress. If he or she gives good service, the usual tip is fifteen percent of the check.

Keep in mind that a little oil of courtesy will save a lot of friction. The spotlight is on teenagers, and you can make your life and the lives of those who know you best very pleasant if you will follow the recommendations of author Elinor Ames, who said, "Good manners follow the laws of common sense and courtesy; bad manners follow the laws of self alone."

5

Pardon Me, Your Maturity Is Showing

THE DICTIONARY defines maturity as ripeness and full development. You are really grown-up when you have a greater desire to pass a geometry exam than the car ahead of you.

Maturity is something that definitely concerns teenagers. Many want to be grown-ups too soon, with equal rights minus the responsibilities. The following tests will help measure how mature you are. Are these things true of you?

1. I can control my temper; I do not sulk, pout, storm, or threaten.
2. I do not bribe, cry, or issue any violent demands to get what I want.
3. I think for myself, and I am fair in evaluating other people's demands.
4. I don't use alibis and excuses when I am a loser.
5. I am not a know-it-all; I understand that other people have rights, too.

There are other tests, too. How about doing things on time? You are not on the mature road if you wait until the last minute to write that English essay or do that little job that Dad asked you to take care of several days ago.

The matter of talking to parents enters in. Mature teenagers do not talk back to their parents. They show respect. Your politeness can boost you toward the head of the class.

Take a good look at your actions in church. Your behavior, your respect, and your worship will add another plus to your record if you have learned to sit up and take notice in the house of the Lord.

The halls of the school are another place to show your stuff in this maturity game. Be respectful of the opposite sex, and learn how to talk with courtesy to your teachers. Eliminate gossip.

Now the tests get tougher. Can you keep money in your pocket without spending it foolishly? Do you dare to stand for high standards and stay true to your convictions?

As you begin working for pay and playing for keeps, I suggest that you:

1. Like your work. (Learn to like it if necessary.)
2. Don't be afraid to do more than you are paid for.
3. Cooperate both with your superiors and coworkers.
4. Have a sensible confidence in yourself and your ability.
5. Cultivate a will to win. If you can't win, help the fellow ahead of you to break the record.

In 1 Corinthians 13:11, the apostle Paul said, "I put away childish things." It would be good to look at some characteristics of children that don't deserve a place in a teen's life.

1. Little children are given to tears.
2. Children love attention. They want the center of the stage.
3. Children take life and its blessings as a matter of course, with little sense of gratitude.

We cannot condemn growing children. Their crowning trait is that they are willing to be taught. They respond to influence and example. But you are growing away from childhood. To refuse to put away childish things is to become a grief to both God and man.

Tomorrow's world belongs to today's teens. It would be tragic for unprepared children to take it over. Mature men and women are needed, and more than that—God-guided men and women. When Christ is your supreme Commander in life, every step is one of blessing and excitement. I challenge you to surrender your will and way to Him, and get your marching orders in prayer from the King of kings at the opening of every day. The prize will go to those who "grow up into him in all things" (Ephesians 4:15).

6

The Great Curfew Battle

THOSE TWO HANDS on the clock can be deadly or a lifesaver—depending on what time is set!

"Why can't I stay out an hour later? Don't you trust me?" If your parents did not trust you, they wouldn't let you go out at all. Your number of evenings out depends on more than showing your parents that they can trust you. They depend on showing your parents that they can trust the safety of the place where you are going, your means of transportation, and the people you will be with during the evening. Your parents want you to have a good time—really! But let's take a quick look at how they feel.

They have years of investment in you. They have given hours of tears, sweat, love, and anxiety in bringing you this far. They read the papers and watch TV, and they can't dis-

miss all the stories about what happens to kids these days. They trust you, but they are extra cautious about how much they trust the other fellow.

This is where you can take over and do some planning, proving, and leveling. Lighten their concern and suspicion by sharing their love and volunteering information. This gives the folks a real sense of relief that your honesty is deeper than the cuff on your shirt. You have nothing to hide.

An unreasonable curfew is often the result of taking parents for granted. Work out all curfew details in advance. It takes two or more for this type of conference, but not more than four! (If your date thinks your folks are unfair or a set of antiques, get him in on the next conference. But don't sit around and let him mouth off at the gruesome twosome.) Don't come by with this stuff that everybody stays out until 2:00 A.M. Your parents' special concern is not everybody, it's you. Therefore, if you want to persuade them to extend a curfew time for you, it is your duty to show them not only that others are doing it, but that what others are doing is right and good for you too. There are very few occasions (if any) that would make a 2:00 A.M. curfew legitimate. Whether we like it or not, the neighbors have eyes and ears. When a Christian teenager has little respect for the graveyard hours, the big eyes of neighbors will look with amazement and suspicion, causing the tongue to wag in question and the head to shake in wonder.

Don't say, "It doesn't matter." It does! As Christians, we are to let our lights shine before men so that they might see our good works and glorify our Father in heaven. A part of our good works is to keep decent hours.

Now back to you and the night! Should you have something to say about the curfew?

Sure! Why not? But say it in the form of information that will help the general and his first lady to be reasonable, thoughtful, and understanding. In this conference, don't talk *at* them. Talk *with* them. Approach the conference table with a positive attitude.

7

Let's Take the "Stew" Out of Students

WHETHER YOU'RE a starry-eyed freshman or a bleary-eyed senior, your school days (or is it *daze*?) have been filled with hours of tough academic studies, as well as fun, friendships, and finals! If high school makes you stew, then chances are it's because you haven't really come to grips with what these school days are all about.

Pack your high school days with everything terrific! Be the best kind of friend and make as many friends as possible. But don't forget that finals come around mighty soon, and in those finals you'll be telling yourself, your teachers, and your parents just what you intend to make out of your life. It's just as important to be a good student as it is to be a good friend. One of these days you'll be standing before someone who can give you the opportunity for a good job, or who can turn you aside and say, "Next, please!" And he won't have to ask too many questions to find out how much you know—and what you do know will depend on how you studied in high school.

I agree, it's hard to study, harder at times than at others, depending on how foggy your mind is or how important some other things are in your life just then. Yes, it could be even harder at times, depending on who the person is occupying your mind when you ought to be studying. But being a student is a big job. It's a job of discipline, and you've got to make up your mind that you're really going to get that lesson. When we see something that we cannot get through our thick heads, something within us shuts off the switch of stick-to-itiveness and we are out like a light. Don't give in!

Did you know that when Walt Disney applied at a Kansas

City newspaper for a job as an artist the editor told him he didn't have any talent, and sent him away urging him to give up art? Don't give up. You can reach your goal if you really want to.

It's important that you study because your future depends on it. If a guy or gal is to get anyplace in life today, he needs an education. And, educations don't come without study. You'll want to be able to look honest men and women straight in the eye. But, more important, you'll want to keep mentally up-to-date with the world in this fast-moving Space Age. You'll want to counsel with a little boy or girl who asks simple questions with big answers. You'll want to get a job to earn a good income. Dig into those books. They are full of what will make you tick.

Being a good student is especially important to the Christian teenager who wants to live a consistent Christian life. You may be the sweetest gal or the kindest guy and the most religious person on campus, but if your marks are not up to or above par, then you might as well join the ostrich and bury your head in the dirt, because the teacher and the other students have every right to snub your religion. Don't be satisfied just to get by. Christian teens should develop one hundred percent of their God-given potential.

Don't complain about too much homework, either. Your teacher gives you credit for being way ahead of the kids twenty years ago and feels that you have the ability to grasp it. You're learning things today which are going to make you leaders in your field tomorrow. Get on the honor roll and remember, that isn't a new kind of Danish pastry.

Action is the only true test of ability. Let's keep at it and make those wheels in the brain prove to the body that we mean business by making successful men and women of ourselves.

I believe the Bible has some pretty sane instruction for all of us. As an old teacher talks to a young pupil in 2 Timothy 2:15, he says, "Study to show thyself approved unto God," that has a meaning both to Christian teens and those who have not found Christ as their Saviour. To the Christian student, he is saying, "Live a life that is clean and purposeful." And to the unsaved student he is saying, "Remember now thy Creator in the days of thy youth."

8

Give It a Fair Trial

M.Y.O.B.

That's all it said on the small piece of paper that was passed down the aisle to Pete in Study Hall 103. After a little probing, he found it came from a friend and meant "mind your own business" in reply to Pete's question, "Are you a Christian?"

What response would you have given?—"I don't know," "What difference does it make?" or "M.Y.O.B."

Oh yes, I agree that there are some people who delight in the popular sport called prying. There are some clods who have the gall to ask questions which are clearly none of their business. You win that point. But let's look at the positive side and call it friendly concern.

When somebody asks you a question that has to do with your life here and your life hereafter, don't blow your cool. It's an important matter.

"OK," you say, "That's your point and I'll answer. I believe I am a Christian because I live in a Christian country. My parents are Christians. I was brought up well, and my parents taught me to behave in a Christian way, so naturally I'm a Christian. I never robbed, cheated, or murdered anyone. I try to treat people the way I expect them to treat me. In my opinion, that's being a Christian. I attend church regularly and give as much as I am able to charities. I think going to church shows you that I am a Christian. There's my answer," you say.

Now it is commendable to go to church and live by the golden rule and try to do what you think is right. Your answer sounds good, but where did you get it? Is it really what you believe? Is it a well-considered decision based on facts?

You may be wrong in your idea of what a Christian is. Since this is such an important matter, listen to a frank challenge.

There is a source book of Christianity. It isn't accepted as a source book by some people, but then a book, like a man, is sometimes given an unfair trial. You are on the jury now. Give the Bible a fair trial. How do you go about it?

1. Read the book for yourself, not just a bit of it. Some por-

tions are difficult. However, there are large portions that anyone can understand with the first reading.

2. Approach the book with an open mind.

3. Read until you get the point. Read it as carefully, and as thoughtfully, and as respectfully as you would read a newspaper or a magazine article.

4. Don't toss it aside because there are words in it you don't understand. Don't quit reading because a portion is dull or seems too frank. Don't get angry because the stories don't seem to turn out the way you think they should.

5. Don't be satisfied with half the evidence. Don't accept and keep in your mind feelings against the Bible without considering that more information might very well change your mind.

6. Take time out to consult with the Author. If there is a God, and if He did write the Bible for you to use as a source book, then it is reasonable to assume that He will bring you to the right understanding about the Bible if you are willing and sincere.

Now a Christian, according to that source book, is a person whose sin has been dealt with by God (Romans 8:1). A Christian is a person who has been received into God's family (John 1:12), who possesses eternal life (John 5:24), who is living a new life (2 Corinthians 5:17), and who loves the Lord Jesus and lives to please Him (John 14:21).

Now, how does that grab you in comparison to the definitions you've heard before? Somewhere along the line we have all heard the word *Christian* used as a synonym for a civilized, democratic, well-behaved, nice, cultured, honest, American church attendant. We cannot believe everything we hear.

Give Christianity a fair trial now. This important decision will affect your life and determine your eternal destiny.

9

Have Life, Will Live

THERE'S NOTHING NEW about making a living! Folks have been doing it for years, and many have been great successes. But living has a stopping point. Life is eternal. Let's get on with the more lasting business of making a life.

There is a circle of young people who know the price of everything and the value of nothing. Life becomes a rat race in which all energy is expended in an effort to get the most out of the short time on earth. Price tags take the place of values. Don't misunderstand me. Making a living is not a small item, especially when everybody around you is doing the same thing in order to live.

But getting what I want today must be the runner-up to getting what I need for eternity. Money is important. So is popularity. I don't want to take any part of success away from you. But never get so concerned with making a living that you lose your life. William Jennings Bryan once said, "Those who live for money spend the first half of their lives getting all they can from everybody else; and the last half trying to keep everybody else from getting what they have got away from them; and they find no pleasure in either half." Life can get to be a merry-go-round if you live it for yourself just to make a living. It becomes a senseless whirl for people who argue that variety is the spice of life and don't have sense enough to know that we cannot live on spice alone.

Things, thrills, and theories are a trio of false estimates of life. Today things may be shining—tomorrow they could be rusty and gone. "A man's life consisteth not in the abundance of things which he possesseth" (Luke 12:15). The things that count and last are focused on the destination of your soul. "For what shall it profit a man, if he shall gain the whole world, and lose his own soul?" (Mark 8:36).

Thrills and pleasures are all related to young people. I am not against having a good time, but be sure to look carefully at the two kinds of pleasure in the Bible. "But she that liveth in pleasure is dead while she liveth" (1 Timothy 5:6), and "At thy right hand there are pleasures for evermore" (Psalm 16:11). Seek the thrills of life Christ gives which give everlasting pleasure.

God says, "heart first," but many are trying to go "head first." Get a good education and investigate theories, but remember that "the world by wisdom knew not God" (1 Corinthians 1:21).

Of course, someone will say, "But there is some truth to it all." Sure, we have an old clock at home that won't run at all and it's still right two times a day! But is that the kind of truth you want? Remember this: "And ye shall know the truth, and the truth shall make you free" (John 8:32). *The* truth is the living Christ! Paul said, "For me to live is Christ" (Philippians 1:21).

Underscore the following considerations. They will help you to make an intelligent decision.

1. Your life is a collection of problems. There are three types: the problem of having, the problem of doing, and the problem of being. The verb *to have* has to do with only one phase of life—the industrial phase, making a living! Making a living is the small, time-serving, dwarfed, paralyzed man's object which touches only the crust of an existence, but it is not the composition of life.

Earth may ask, "What have you?" Heaven may ask, "What did you?" But God will ask, "What are you?" God's big word is *be*. Daniel Webster said, "You can work upon marble but it will perish; upon brass but time will efface it; rear temples but they will crumble in the dust." Invest your life in Christ and you will never regret it.

2. Your life is an investment. Since you have only one life to live and it is surprisingly brief, your great concern should be how to invest it. Are you going to be a miser and only give the tiniest share of yourself, or are you going to invest everything for Jesus Christ who promises abundant life?

3. Your life is a probation. This implies three things: time, choice, and destiny.

Time is short. When you stop to consider that we spend one-third of that time in sleep, another third in infancy and preparation for our life's work, it leaves a very small amount of time for the real making of a life. It is smart and right to give your heart to Christ in your teen years.

Choice is a momentous thing. A choice results in an action; consistent actions result in a habit; a habit results in a character; a character results in a destiny. "Choose ye this day whom ye will serve" (Joshua 24:15).

You settle your own destiny in life. Everybody who goes with the lost world goes on his own feet, in his own shoes, by his own choice against the will of God. Your destiny depends on your decision. God has provided a way and given Jesus Christ. Heaven can be yours. Salvation is a free gift. You decide what you want.

4. Your life can be a failure or a success. You can make a good living and still be a failure. We stand back and admire aggressive, successful people. But everything fades into oblivion and is crushed under the feet of a fast-moving world when no plans are made for making a life.

Life without Christ is a hopeless jigsaw puzzle. Don't go around forever blowing bubbles, looking for ships that never come in, or chasing pots of gold at the ends of vanishing rainbows. You will find really satisfying life when you trust Christ. Eternal life is available to those who will take it. Acknowledge the Saviour today and believe Him. Confess your sins and come to Him just now. Life in Christ is longer than time. It is eternal.

10

Fussy Flossie and Sensible Sam

YOUR CHARACTER and career are at stake! The community has its eye not only on you, but on the gang you run around with. Your friends are mighty important people when others are making a judgment of your character. So investigate wisely when choosing companions.

You may be called Fussy Flossie if you are careful about how you select your friends, but folks will come to realize that you aren't stuck-up if you have an attractive personality. You will be admired if you refuse to be in the company of those who have no respect for their elders, talk lightly of home and parents, or tell shady stories. Staying away from questionable pastimes and places may win you the title of fussy or old-fashioned, but a good reputation is highly valuable.

Join the side of Sensible Sam. He's no sissy, but he takes care in his selection of friends. He's polite and courteous, participates in school activities, and is known for his fairness. But you won't find him involved in vandalism or lazy loitering.

Here are some questions you might ask yourself before becoming fast friends:

1. How are his speech and attitude? Is he respectful when talking about his parents and teachers? Does he use profanity? Is he courteous to the opposite sex?

2. How does he spend his spare time? Does he take time to be with his family? Is he cooperative in the activity of the home? Does he have constructive hobbies or does he waste time? Is he spending his time in places that you know are wrong or questionable?

3. Does he attend church faithfully? Look out for anyone

who talks slightingly about the church as if it were out-of-date. Be careful about little people who are trying to be tough in impressing you that church is for children and old women.

4. What are the reputations of his friends? It may sound as if this is drawing fine points and getting fussy, but it is extremely important in life that you select a companion who is not involved with others that you could never approve of.

5. Does he have any ambitions for the future? The best way to find out is to ask him. Be careful about anyone who has determined to be nothing.

You are classified with those in whose company you are seen. Be smart. Investigate wisely.

11

Down Lover's Lane

GOD HAS A PURPOSE for your life, and there may be in His plan
a person who can enrich your life and bring you joy. Christians
are not just blind creatures in a world of blind chance. Some
men say they are self-made men, but usually they show such
poor architectural skill that anyone would know that they
lack God in their lives.

God has a wonderful plan for Christians. Despite the tangled
threads, the jumble of design and color, there is a clear, beautiful pattern for each life; and only when you reach the end of
the way can you appreciate the design God has created especially for you.

The first and most important step in realizing God's plan for
you is salvation. Your courtship problems take on a different
light as a Christian. Your choice as a believer is limited. You
must be careful whom you choose to be your companions. I
would seriously question any dating with those of unlike faiths.
The old idea of thinking you will be able to win him or her to
the Lord after marriage has been disproved many times.

In your courtship what really counts? Just what does a guy
look for in a girl?

It is beauty—not just physical beauty, but beauty of character. The truth is that ninety-five percent of the girls are not
flawlessly beautiful, as they all have an assortment of freckles,
knock-knees, pug noses, and other minor imperfections. Beauty
that comes from within the heart is the kind that lasts long
after the bloom of youth has faded. It is no special credit to a
girl to have a lovely face and be considered beautiful at the
age of sixteen, but a woman of forty who has qualities of love-

liness that have come from a strong character and a life of clean living is to be highly esteemed. Her beauty didn't just happen. It was cultivated.

Look for the beauty of unselfishness. You may find a plain, unglamorous girl who will assume a quiet loveliness in years to come when you hear her old slippers clopping down the chilly hallway to tend a sick child. The outward beauty that can be rubbed off or washed off is not comparable to the inner radiance that comes from a girl who puts others first and strives to make a happy home for her husband. Look for the beauty of kindness and enthusiasm.

Wait a minute, fellows. What do you think a girl looks for when considering a prospective mate? If she is wise, she will observe things that will count over a period of time—genuine courage, courtesy, respect, ambition, and thoughtfulness. A fellow can have a dozen faults, but any girl will overlook them if he is, above all, considerate.

Fellows, remember this—your treatment of your girl reveals your character. As a Christian, remember that you belong to Someone else. You are not your own. Your eyes are not yours to be used improperly. Your lips are not yours to cheapen with passing love interests. Your hands are not yours to use in careless caresses. Your heart is not yours to throw around freely. An evening of necking or making out is off limits for Christians. It soils the mind and stains your soul. The current philosophy that everyone should get what he wants, regardless of right or wrong, is the devil's own lie from the pit of hell.

Remember that success may be getting what you want, but happiness is really wanting what you get. Multitudes of people today are frustrating themselves in a mad effort to get what they want, and then after they have knocked themselves out getting it, they find they aren't happy with it.

1. Don't be gold diggers. Some girls marry for keeps, all right —they keep asking for furs, keep asking for money, keep asking for trinkets. A girl who can't enjoy a hamburger and insists on an expensive steak with trimmings isn't the kind who will

make her budget stretch through the week. A girl who is considerate of her date's wallet can provide good companionship over a coke or enjoy taking a walk, without flattening a fellow's allowance for the week.

2. Be considerate of your parents. Let them know where you are and when you will be home! Introduce them to your date. Most fellows are proud of girls who have curfew hours! A fellow who insists on breaking them or disregarding your parents' wishes isn't the kind to continue dating.

3. Don't cheapen yourself by giving in to an evening of necking and letting down the standards you want to keep. No self-respecting fellow wants a girl who has been manhandled by every fellow she has been out with. The Scriptures tell us, in 1 Timothy 5:22, "Keep thyself pure." That means in all phases of your life.

4. Share your problems with your girlfriend or boyfriend. Observe how he or she accepts responsibility. Learn what things about you there are that might cause undue criticism or problems in the future. Do you have habits that are annoying to each other?

5. Try to cultivate the characteristics in your own life which will suit you for marriage. Be prayerful about it and ask God to give you the ability to develop some of these qualities. When considering a mate, look for one who is kind, tactful, agreeable, generous, thoughtful, honest, patient, loving, steady, and willing to learn. (Make sure though that if that person says he runs his life on a budget, he doesn't mean fussbudget.) Make certain that he or she loves God above all and is seeking to please Him. Select someone who has a clean, orderly mind. Be sure he shows a genuine interest in God's Word. Watch out for anyone who becomes surly or disagreeable when reversals come. It has been said that a man can walk a mile with an adoring sweetheart and not be tired, but to walk a block with a nagging wife can exhaust him.

In your courtship, temptation will come. The Lord can purify your hearts and prepare you to face them. Remember, when you meet up with temptation, turn to the Lord and you will find the way. Let me give you three weapons from Scripture to fight temptation:

1. Courageous joy—"Count it all joy when ye fall into divers temptations" (James 1:2). Don't gripe, complain or grumble.
2. Counterattack—"Overcome evil with good" (Romans 12:21).
3. Constant vigilance—"Be vigilant" (1 Peter 5:8).

Here is a prayer written by a fifteen-year-old girl asking the Lord's guidance in her dating life:

> Dear Lord,
>
> I pray that You will grant me the patience to wait. Somewhere there is waiting for me, one chosen by You, who shall be my mate. Will he possess the characteristics of passion, humor, humility, kindness, and love? Will he be able to get up when knocked down by the pounding waves of life? Will he comfort and guide me through our life together as man and wife? Will he look with joyful love and awe upon our gift from You whenever it may come, our newborn child? Will he look at me with love as I lie beside him each night? Will he be there to gently brush away the doubts and fears which bring tears to my eyes, all because of life? Will he be there to laugh with me over each joy that You give to us? Will he love You, God? Will he say "I believe" each time he hears his child laugh or sees the sky or feels the falling rain? Yes, dear Lord, he will be there because he will be a child of Yours. Please, dear Lord, grant me the patience to wait. I believe the man that You have chosen for me somewhere waits.

12

Mighty Man or Measly Mouse?

STAND FOR THE RIGHT. It may cost you something, but what you receive is the best bargain you ever had. God is the Judge of what is right and what is wrong. As His child, you are a member of royalty, and those who really count will look to you to stand fast for all things which are right. But what is right?

1. It is right to stand fast and firm for the faith revealed in the Scriptures. Don't let anyone pierce your thinking or dent your shield when it comes to standing firm for Jesus Christ, His

death, His burial, His resurrection, and His coming again. The Bible gives you the answers and the positive assurance that it is right to believe that Jesus Christ was crucified, buried, and risen again according to the Scriptures.

2. It is right to be honest. A cheat is always discovered. His red face and fumbling fingers soon spell out to all in his presence that he is hiding something from someone. Don't turn your back on your mother or dad by being dishonest in any act or deed. Don't be the thief of someone's character or someone's time. Be honest in the classroom, in the community, in the church. Be honest with God.

Don't pull someone else down in order to pull yourself up. It is always right to tell the truth no matter what the price. God looks with favor upon those who have learned the art of truth.

3. It is right to stand for your convictions, providing these convictions are based upon God's best when you are confronted with a choice. Remember, men argue for opinions but die for convictions.

4. It is right to honor your father and mother. It is extremely important that you learn to take orders, since someday you will be in the position of giving them yourself. Someday you will want the respect that we are asking you to give always to Mother and Dad. Remember this is the first commandment with promise.

5. It is right to rebuke those who take the name of the Lord in vain. Never let anyone speak disgracefully of the Lord whether it be in the presence of ladies or gentlemen.

All right now, show your colors! Keep the standards flying high, and you will discover soon that you will be looked upon as one who has a sense of direction and purpose.

Now look me right in the eye! Are you a mighty man or a measly mouse?

13

Meek Molly and Wavering Willy

WHEN CHRISTIAN TEENS are challenged and ridiculed, Meek Molly and Wavering Willy are the spineless characters who whine to their friends and family, "Oh, it's *so* hard to live the Christian life. I can't take this persecution another day! Do I have to put up with this ridicule?"

Look at some examples from the Bible. Jeremiah took discouragement, but he bounced right back up to the top of the heap. Have you ever been persecuted like the three Hebrew boys who were thrown into the fiery furnace? They didn't give up, because they had a companion in there with them who wouldn't permit the flames to burn anything but the ropes that tied them. And let's not forget the example of Jesus. Whole crowds laughed at Him.

Then what about the crowd that's laughing at you? Remember, when you stand fast for Christ, even in the midst of ridicule, the crowd will show a greater respect for you and your Lord even as they did when those three boys marched out of the furnace!

If you're never ridiculed, I fear you aren't living too close to the Lord. However, every time you stand up for what you believe, you'll find that each succeeding remark will give you increased stamina and courage to keep going on.

The mockers need a real jolt, and they'll get it from a clean-cut Christian who will show himself above average by taking it for Christ and never letting down the bars of compromise.

Remember these rules; or better still, write them on a piece of paper and insert them in your Bible and class books. Here's how to meet ridicule:

1. Don't show alarm; it's going to happen.
2. Don't defend yourself with anger.
3. Never fight ridicule with ridicule.
4. Don't be apologetic.
5. Stand up to it; you will be the target every time if you run from ridicule now.
6. Don't be odd, but don't be afraid to be different.
7. Always declare yourself. Be on the offensive.
8. Be thoughtful and understanding.
9. Be bright and optimistic.
10. Be loyal to your Lord.

I don't mean to leave you with the impression that you are to be the doormat for anyone. I don't think you ever will after the gang finds out that you have something worthwhile and you mean to stick by it. Keep your heart in tune with heaven, your eyes looking upward, and your burden ever increased for the students in your school whose destination without Christ will be eternal fire.

Remember that the message you're to give out is a loving, kind, thoughtful word from the very lips and heart of Jesus as He speaks and says, "I am come that they might have life, and that they might have it more abundantly" (John 10:10).

You needn't be a Meek Molly or a Wavering Willy. Let your firmness shine with Christian kindness.

14

Snobs!

"I LIKE MY CHURCH!" This is one of the most refreshing statements to come from the lips of a young teen in a midwestern town. But what do others think about your church and you?

I invited a couple of sharp teens to join us for special meeting in a church with a reputation for being "on the ball," only to be thrown for a loss with the stern statement, "Not me! Those kids are a big, disgusting clique."

Cliques keep others away. They promote suspicion and give a bad name to the pastor and other church leaders. Young people are too often guilty of gathering in a corner with an exclusive, snobbish attitude. This is a symbol of pride and the concern that if others were to be included in a circle of close-knit friends, someone will have to give up his popularity and influence (if he had any to begin with).

The word *snob* sends pin pricks dashing up and down my spine. Christian young people are reminded that our only proper glory is in the cross of Christ.

Friendliness is a part of teen living. The art of having many friends is learned by recognizing that there is something important about everyone. Look at the truly popular people. You find them among a variety of groups and interests.

This becomes even more important in the church. Folks in the church need encouragement. The people outside the church need friends who can show them a true representation of the Christian life by their words and actions.

Have a lot of friends. Of course there are special friends, and I would not want this taken away. We are bound to like certain people better than others. Why not? Some deserve it. But don't wear a clique label. It hurts you and your church and its influence. Show your Christian maturity by getting rid of those things that may appear snobbish to those who don't know you. Show interest in those outside your circle of closest friends. Stay clear of the trap of self-centeredness by practicing the presence of Christ in your life at all times.

One Monday morning a high school girl wrote the following letter to a friend:

I attended your church yesterday. Although you had invited me only once, I felt you were sincere in wanting me to come. I looked for you, hoping to sit beside you. But you were not there.

A stranger, I wanted to sit near the back of the church. But I couldn't. Those rows were all packed. An usher had to lead me right up to the front. I felt as if I were on parade.

The congregation sang hymns that I didn't know. I tried to mumble along and pretend that I was singing, but I had never heard those hymns before. I must confess that I was surprised to note that some of the church people weren't singing. Between their sighs and yawns they just stared into space. Three of the kids that I had respected on campus were whispering to one another. Another girl was giggling. I really didn't expect that in your church.

The pastor's sermon was interesting, although some members of the choir didn't seem to think so. They looked bored and restless. One kept smiling at someone in the congregation. The pastor spoke about the reality of faith. The message got to me, and I made up my mind to speak to someone about it after the service. But utter chaos reigned after the benediction.

I said good morning to one couple, but their greeting was less than cordial. I looked for some teens with whom I could discuss the sermon, but they were huddled in a corner, talking about the newest records. One girl looked my way but just waved.

My parents don't go to church. I came alone yesterday hoping to find a friendly congregation in which they wouldn't feel too out of place.

But as I left, I wasn't too impressed with the sign outside the church that read, "The Friendly Church with the Warm Welcome." I'm sorry, but I won't be back.

15

Don't Fence Them In—Or Out

"LOVE THY NEIGHBOR as thyself." Did you ever think of how much love that is that you're supposed to give to your neighbor? Don't kid yourself—this is a tall order. Most of us love ourselves quite a lot. We think we're pretty special. We're commanded by God to love our neighbor *that* much!

Who is your neighbor? He's the guy or gal next door who wears better threads than you do and the one on the other side who isn't as cool as your special friends. The couple across the street that put up a "Keep Off the Grass" sign and the local senior citizens who complain so much about noise are your neighbors, too. Neighbors take on all sorts of characteristics. They may not see eye to eye with you on the importance of church, or they may be religious fanatics.

In Proverbs 3:27, we see another description of proper treatment of neighbors. "Withhold not good from them to whom it is due, when it is in the power of thine hand to do it." But to whom is good due? How about that catty blonde with the smutty reputation who sits next to you in history class? Could that tight sweater possibly hide a broken heart? And what about that guy in your class who is visited more frequently by the truant officer than the Sunday school teacher? Could a life like his ever be worthwhile to Jesus? You know it could be—Christ transforms lives.

Let's take a quick glance at the good Samaritan. He was "moved with compassion" by his sharp eye and soft heart. He didn't ask about the wounded man's race or background or education. That wounded man was his neighbor.

It would have been easy for him to look at the situation from

the other side of the street and say as the others had, "He should have known better than to walk through that haven for hoodlums! He's had it. Maybe he'll learn a lesson from this experience."

But the good Samaritan saw a fellowman in need and was willing to spend time, effort, and money to meet that need.

Instead of talking about love, let's demonstrate it.

Sometimes I cringe when I hear people sing with chests out, heads up, and voices loud, "We shall come rejoicing, bringing in the sheaves." I look around and ask, "Where are the sheaves? Where are your neighbors?"

"He that goeth forth and weepeth, bearing precious seed, shall doubtless come again with rejoicing, bringing in the sheaves" (Psalm 126:6). I see five important lessons here for myself as well as you:

1. *Going*. That's action. Give legs to your Christianity. Express your burden.

2. *Weeping*. The tears show you really mean what you're praying about. I heard a girl say to her father, "Daddy, if you don't get saved tonight, I'm going to die. I've prayed for you, and I can't go on." I watched that same father who hadn't been in church for fifteen years walk to the front of the church,

grab the hand of the pastor, and say, "If what my girl has causes her to be that concerned about me, I want to meet her Jesus."

3. *Bearing.* Take the incorruptible seed of the Word of God to your neighbors. It's the only way to bring forth fruit. Relay John 5:24.

4. *Rejoicing.* I can hear the apostle Paul reminding us to "Rejoice, and again I say, rejoice." A lifeguard at a beach told us some time ago, "The reason I'm so happy today is because I just rescued a little nine-year-old girl from drowning."

5. *Bringing.* Notice that this verse begins with action and closes with action plus harvest.

Now let's go back to our neighbor. Don't fence him in or fence him out with racial, academic, denominational, or social barriers.

Well, yes, it's "duck soup" on paper, but it's hard to put into action. But we are instructed to be concerned about others. Self-centeredness reveals immaturity and produces selfish citizens. The razor edge of what I'm getting at probes our prejudices. We hang too much on the limb of ambition and pride. "Birds of a feather flock together," but we do not win by isolation. Remember Matthew 5:16, "Let your light so shine before men that they might see your good works and glorify your Father which is in heaven."

We'll visit our neighbor when he is in financial need. We'll stand by him in his sorrow. We'll be glad to give him a cup of sugar.

Now, look at your neighbors again in the light of their spiritual needs. They aren't going to get too mad at you if you go in the spirit of love and interest and sharing. Instead of taking the parable of the good Samaritan and applauding the hero and slapping him on the back to the tune of "For He's A Jolly Good Fellow," let me enunciate again the punch line, "You go and do the same." Share the incomparable joy of salvation by grace through faith.

16

That Giant Called Fear

A RUGGED, tough football player admitted that he was so afraid of the dark that he slept with his light on every night. I counseled with a teenager the other day who admitted that she was afraid to wake up and go outside for fear of what might happen that day.

You can call this the Aspirin Age or the Computer Age, if you like, but in the heart of many this is the Age of Fear.

Most people battle with the giant called fear. It goes beyond the fears about job security, health, and acceptance. It is the fear of meeting the everyday demands of life.

Come to grips with fear at once and realize it is the tool of the devil to keep you from a happy walk and relationship with Christ. It narrows your vision. It produces resentment, sometimes hate. It lowers your resistance and brings frustration. Fear makes your imagination run wild and you become an unhappy pessimist. If the devil puts the ring of fear in your nose he can lead you wherever he wills.

Christians, let's get with it. The "fear nots" of the Bible are exciting and strong foundations. "Fear ye not, stand still, and see the salvation of the Lord" (Exodus 14:13). "The Lord is my light and my salvation; whom shall I fear? The Lord is the strength of my life; of whom shall I be afraid?" (Psalm 27:1). "The fear of man bringeth a snare: but whoso putteth his trust in the Lord shall be safe" (Proverbs 29:25). "Say to them that are of a fearful heart, Be strong, fear not" (Isaiah 35:4).

If you want victory against the giant of fear, follow these three steps:

Step One: Learn to love. "God hath not given us the spirit of

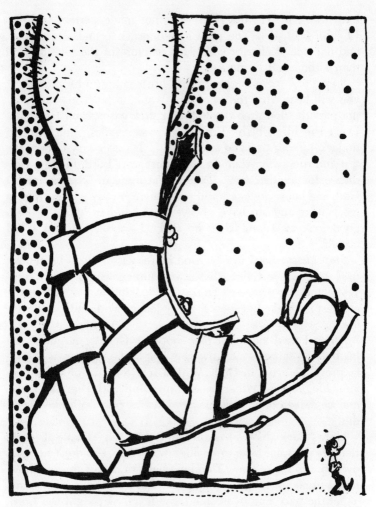

fear, but of power, and of love, and of a sound mind" (2 Timothy 1:7). I heard the other day, "I fear that nobody loves me." My reply was very simple as I said, "Perhaps it is because you do not love." It is not all take, a lot of it is give. "There is no fear in love; but perfect love casteth out fear: because fear hath torment. He that feareth is not made perfect in love" (1 John 4:18, 19). You must love in order to understand love, and one act of charity will teach us more of the love of God than a thousand sermons.

Step Two: Examine yourself. This is going to be exciting if you will hear what the Lord God wants to tell you. You may not pass the first time through, but stick with it and try again. Don't run like Elijah. He ran seventeen miles, then stopped under a juniper tree and asked to die. It's very easy to take the test and run away when you fail. Just say, "Lord, I'll be a candidate for another try." Take the attitude of "Search me, O God, and know my heart and see if there be any wicked way in me." Fear and sin have always gone hand in hand. Take a good look at Adam when he said, "I was afraid and I hid myself."

Step Three: Look up. "If God be for us, who can be against us?" Joshua and Caleb, those two courageous soldiers who investigated the promised land, were looking to God while the other spies looked at giants. They looked with faith, not with flesh.

When David looked at nine-foot-nine Goliath, he didn't see his bulging muscles and towering height, he just saw a chance to prove his trust in God. With a fear the size of Goliath in your life, you can either be swallowed up with everybody else and be defeated, or you can stand fast in your faith like David did.

Here's your chance to prove to a doubting, skeptical world that life does not have to be filled with fear. You don't need an overdose to shake fear. You don't have to run. You don't have to get stoned or take a drug trip that has a high risk of crashing.

Set the pace and overcome those fears. "I sought the Lord, and he heard me, and delivered me from all my fears" (Psalm 34:4). "Peace I leave with you, my peace I give unto you: not as the world giveth, give I unto you. Let not your heart be troubled, neither let it be afraid" (John 14:27).

17

The Dropouts

I'VE JUST REVIEWED some of the reasons that teenagers have given me for leaving the church. Here they are in the order of frequency:

"The church doesn't offer enough activities."

"Church is too often boring and irrelevant."

"School activities keep me too busy to get involved at church."

"My parents don't care whether I go to church."

"None of my friends go to church, so why should I?"

"I have to work on Sundays."

"I prefer to watch TV."

"I can't swallow some of the doctrines that the church insists on."

"The kids at church are an unfriendly clique."

"I have no way to get to church."

Are those reasons or excuses? I grant that some of these may be legitimate, but it puzzles me that we can find so many reasons to stay away from God's house that we do not use for other places.

An unfriendly nurse would not keep us from going to the hospital if we really needed medical care. Disagreeing with the coach would not keep us off the team. And a lot of other activities wouldn't keep us from meeting the gang at the pizza shop.

It bothers me that so many young people drop out of church. Experts say that more people leave the church at the age of sixteen than at any other age. One survey reported that fifty percent were between eleven and fourteen, and twenty-four percent were eighteen or over.

I'm convinced that there are thousands of teens who want a spiritual challenge and who are interested in God's way for their lives. I agree that pastors and other church leaders need to check up on their ministry to youth. One dropout said, "Pastors don't preach on subjects that are vital to young people." Another complained, "It's always the same old thing. We're never challenged." These statements indicate to me that teenagers will stay in the church if the church is willing to minister to their real needs.

Stick with your church and continue to practice your faith. Get involved in its program. When you are willing to take one step forward, it's easier to suggest to somebody else to take a step forward also. Be constantly aware of your responsibility to share the Saviour with others.

Don't make excuses for yourself any longer. Go to church and look for something good. It may surprise you what you will find!

When teenagers put their shoulders to the wheel and make up their minds to be something and to do something, action will become the true test of ability. When you stand shoulder to shoulder, wanting to make your church the best in town for the glory of God, a soul-saving center of aggressive evangelism, then and only then, can you expect your pastor, your parents, and your deacons to line up with you and march forward to the credit of the gospel.

18

Watch for a Happening

I SAY A LOT of good things about the church because I know many good churches that are really on the ball. I frequently come face to face with young people who are causing a real happening in their church. Revival is no longer just a word; it is being put into action. Instead of complaining about what's wrong with the church members, the young people that are involved in revival are examining themselves. You can improve the situation in your church by being on the *in* better than you can by being on the *out*.

All right, you've said it and so have I, "There are too many hypocrites in the church." One fellow was complaining about this problem when he was advised by a quick-witted friend, "If you ever find a perfect church, don't go in because it won't be perfect anymore when you enter."

A London church found it necessary to post this notice: "Not everyone who goes to this church is converted. Watch your hat and coat!"

I remember having the feeling of distaste with the church, and I must be honest that I still have a little problem from time to time. The only trouble, though, with staying away from church because of dislikes is that there is no way to continue constructive conversation with those who are involved on the other side of ideas and practices that obviously matter a great deal. As a member of the young world, you are beginning to think as an adult. Many of the things that you are finding distasteful are what you experienced as a child in the church. Wouldn't it be more reasonable to take your thinking and your feelings into the sanctuary each Sunday and test them out for the next few years? If you stay at home, you don't have anybody to discuss your grievances with, or test your ideas against, or any way to get fresh insight, so you're left with only unhappy childhood memories.

It's easy to sit in Row D, seat 35, in the grandstand and yell at the quarterback for calling the wrong play. Get on the playing field and make the first team. Get into the church and make your influences felt.

Ask for a job. Stay on praying ground. Get involved in the calling program. Read your Bible. Have an active prayer list. Share your faith with at least one person a day. Then when you have something to say, people will listen to you. A teenager mentioned to me the other day that she was tired of her pastor. I recommended she have a conference with him at once and tell him what she had told me and *why* she was tired of him. The right kind of minister will listen with both ears, and you may leave that session with a new appreciation and a new insight for the work of the church.

Whenever there are people involved, you are bound to think that some are really "out of it." You don't improve the situation, though, by underscoring that crowd in your thinking. Bridge it, by "forsaking not the assembling of yourselves together."

Go to church next Sunday after having spent fifteen minutes in prayer before you walk out your front door. Then check to make sure you have your Bible and notebook. Take notes on the pastor's message, then perhaps you should preach it back to yourself, then back to him.

Watch for a happening in your life and in his!

19

Tough but True

ONE OF MY FATHER'S most dramatic statements was, "I mean business." It was really frustrating as I grew up to realize that, in spite of the fact that I weighed twenty pounds more than my father when I was a high school senior, he wasn't afraid of me. Not even my mother at a hundred and thirty pounds was afraid of me. Her famous statement was, "I'm talking to you. Now listen."

A college professor once remarked to me, "Your parents should not have said that because they could have warped your personality." My answer was, "My father didn't care if he warped me. He just meant business. And we turned out pretty well!"

As you read the Bible, you will come to one account after another where God meant business.

Take the account of Moses. God called him to lead the en-

tire nation of Israel out of bondage in Egypt. The fourth chapter of Exodus gives us the objections Moses had to carrying out God's will. He complained that the people were unbelieving and that he was a poor speaker. But God meant business! He gave Moses the power to perform miraculous signs of God's power and assured him that He would teach him what to say. So Moses obeyed.

Or look at the apostle Paul in the New Testament. When his story began, his name was Saul. He didn't argue that he was ill equipped to serve God; he was spending all his energy killing Christians. But God meant business. Saul was dramatically converted and spent the rest of his life proclaiming the gospel.

God still means business today. There is no place for a "ho-hum" attitude toward the development of your abilities. He wants your talent, your life, your personality. You are important to Him. Give the best and make the most out of what you have been given.

A senior class displayed this motto not long ago. "What you are is God's gift to you; what you become is your gift to God." God means business when He invites you to come and believe. He means business when He assures you of everlasting life and forgiveness of sins. He means business when He asks you to walk in the light even as He is in the light. He means business when He asks you to present your body a living sacrifice. He means business when He invites us to go out into the highways and byways and compel others to come to Him too.

But God does not just demand obedience. He supplies the power you need to accomplish His will. He means business when He says, "I will never leave thee, nor forsake thee" (Hebrews 13:5).

When God means business with you, remember the assurance of the apostle Paul which is true for all believers: "I can do all things through Christ which strengthenth me" (Philippians 4:13).

DON'T CLOSE THE BOOK NOW. The remaining chapters will help those who can help you.

The establishment (if you prefer to call it that) put a 747 in the air, found a cure for polio, and put a man on the moon. They are not so dumb. The more they know about you, the more able they will be to help you to accomplish even more than they did.

Let's communicate. Share these chapters with those close to you.

20

The Generation Gasp

or

How to Live with Your Teenager and Like It

"My folks don't understand me."

"They worry too much."

"They forget what it's like to be a teenager."

If this sounds like a gripe session, you guessed it right. And it's about you in Parentsville! I tuned in to the now crowd as they discussed their homes and came to the conclusion that parents are important people.

These real characters who belong to you are exciting humans, and no one can help them as well as you. They tax your patience but seldom mean to do so. They are human dynamos when they are with their friends at school but often too tired to move when asked to mow the lawn or dry the dishes.

We have listened to society call them swingers, rollers, hipsters, the restless ones, the curled lip generation, and the sound searchers. Often we have joined in with the opposition like the way-outs and the quiet ones. We look around and see some beards, beads, and boots, so we write the word *teenager* in big letters in our mind. Frustrated arms start waving, the hermit spirit comes over us, and we wonder "What next?"

But the overwhelming majority of the teenagers are staunchly committed, worthwhile people who can make your life pleasant.

What about the gap? Is there one? If so, hooray! There needs to be a natural generation gap. It is too often confused with the generated gaps like sensitivity, credibility, and compatibility. We can correct the misconception by finding out what the teenager expects of his parents. He doesn't always feel that you have to "take the rap for the gap," as spelled out in this letter:

> I believe the generation gap doesn't have to exist. I am now seventeen, and until this year my parents and I were involved in the gap. It was my fault. I never told them anything about my social life, or anything else, for that matter.

Here is another teen opinion: "I think that the generation gap is just part of a larger gap—the gap between people."

How can we best help them? When do you lay aside the woodshed approach for the heart-to-heart talk? When do you lay down the "lickin'" stick for the no-privilege order? Teenagers have underscored some principles that are among the things they appreciate in the adults who can keep them from being the "untouchables" or the "unbearables."

1. Don't be afraid to speak up. Be ready to tell your teenagers when you think they are wrong. This is your right and duty, and the earlier in life you do it, the easier you'll get through to them when they get older. But remember, say it in a tone of voice you'd want to hear.

2. Expect excitement. Put on your shock-proof jacket. Be ready for the hair-raising stuff and the burst and blast of the twentieth century go-getter. Your lovable tax exemptions are victims of the cult of immediacy, and we need to hear them out. Understanding counsel is in order, not steady diets of severe lectures.

3. Be firm with affection. Teens expect and appreciate limits. Even the ones who complain the loudest like to have rules. The son who argues, "Everyone else is going!" may secretly be glad he has an out. One girl thanked her father for the curfew. "I am grateful for a check valve," she said. Be consistent in enforcing discipline, and when you make a rule, abide by it.

4. Don't expect them to be perfect. Don't talk about your report card. Grandma may come to Junior's side. Accept the fact that each child is a little different than you are now and that things have changed. Guide and guard with a praying

heart, and expect them to have a couple of bumps here and there.

5. Make their friends welcome at home. Look and act like parents. Don't be a super snooper in teen affairs when the gang comes over for pizza and pop. Be conveniently available. Never humiliate your teenagers by a dressing down before their friends. Avoid sarcasm and do all of your character quizzing about their friends in private.

6. Don't forget to pat them on the back. The teen years are doing and going years. Show interest in what is going on. When they do something well, say, "Nice work, I'm proud of you." Spend more time encouraging the good than in punishing the bad.

7. Give them time to be alone. This is often a good tonic, for it gives them time to think things through. Respect their wish for privacy. Don't go barging into their room without knocking first. They don't mind being told what they ought to do (most of the time) but as one teen put it, "Once we've been told, we want to be on our own. We want our parents to expect the best of us, not fear the worst."

8. Keep the lines of communication open. Maybe teenagers don't even understand themselves, but they want parents to whom they can go and who they can be sure will at least listen and let them explain. The hardest thing to give is *in*. We cut the line of communication with interruptions. Keep in mind that "an open ear drinks dry a thousand tongues." Don't laugh off any problem with an attitude of "it will blow over" or "they will grow out of it."

9. Keep learning. Your young people expect you to know. If you don't, find out real soon! A surprising number of high school students complain about their parents' cultural deficiencies and their seeming indifference to developments in the world. Look at the satisfying but proud startle in your offspring when you come up with something he doesn't know. Do it often, even daily. And then, don't brag about it.

10. Stand by them, not over them. Show quiet concern for

what they wear and where they go. Prepare them to lead *their* lives, not yours. You are the commander-in-chief of the household and they will sense your consistent leadership. Stand by. They want guidance, but don't keep nagging about every little thing. That's what they told me to tell you!

11. Make them feel wanted. It is easy at times to knowingly act aloof and ignore the one you love. Give assignments with directions and know-how to fulfill them. Show confidence in their potential, and don't judge until the job has been fulfilled or neglected.

12. Never let your love be doubted. Do not put conditions on giving affection. Do not engage in a blow-by-blow verbal exchange with your teens on how much love they owe you because you have done so much for them. Just keep demonstrating your love. This is maturity that is contagious.

13. Give direct answers to direct questions. Tell it like it is. Say it with loving conviction. Hems and haws are for cowards. If you don't know the answer, say so. Then look it up. Answer with the same frankness with which you were asked the question. Be bold but kind. Give your opinion with crisp and sincere conviction. In all probability you will be quoted.

14. Call a family conference. Give your teenagers a chance to be heard and show their stuff. Ask their opinions on matters of family concern and interest. Treat them as junior partners in the firm. Exercise some practical flexibility with the art of give-and-take. Explain that junior's taking over the wheel causes an increase in the insurance rate. Teach them to pray with a prayer list of mutual family concern and involvements. Talk *with* each other, not *at* each other.

15. Be shining examples. Look at your own conduct on and off home base. Don't argue with your mate in front of the family. Don't gossip. Talk things over in a daily conference with the Lord. Display a life that reveals the result of a daily quiet time and separation unto the Lord. Organize and maintain a daily family worship. This will teach your family the importance of family living and prayer. Read your Bible. Lead

the way to Sunday school, church, and prayer meeting. Be out in front of the family with a banner, not behind with a whip. "Let's go" should take the place of "get going." Don't prohibit without providing.

Your young people are living in a world that is seeking escape from pressure and showing revolt against some of our materialistic value judgments. At times they are as mixed up as a termite in a yo-yo. You have a big investment in them. Your sons and daughters are smart enough to see foundation love that is sincere and discipline which is for their own good. God wants your home to be blessed with happiness and unity. Every teenager has a right to have a house that is a home. We need to supply them with vital needs, and they are not provided through overpermissiveness or overindulgence. Our chief job is to recognize and identify their needs, then meet them with courage, understanding, trust, discipline, and conviction. When you back your parental role of responsibility with dedicated living and a shining example, your tax exemptions will look with respect and not fear or rebellion upon the important twosome who have found the way, are pointing to it, and walking in it.

No one can help your teenager the way you can if you stick to your job, blending love and good sense with firmness.

21

Reach Them—Then Keep Them

Here are some practical tips to help you get along with young people in your church:

1. Never stop being a student. You should be willing to learn in order to keep up-to-date with this fast-moving, educated teen crowd. Keep up with current events, modern fashions, and school activities. No one will find it out sooner than your young people if you are not prepared. Dig into new things. Read new books.

2. Accentuate the positive. Be progressive in your preaching, in your attitudes, and in your ways. Always be prepared to constructively counsel your young people by recommending something healthfully aggressive in the place of those things they shouldn't be toying with.

3. Eliminate the ego. Quit talking about yourself. You are dealing with a crowd who rubs shoulders with an army of egotists every day. Don't be weak, but be humble. Remember John 3:30: "He must increase, but I must decrease."

4. Stay on praying ground. In a discussion panel some time ago, four teenagers agreed that the pastor that appealed to them most was the man who could pray. You must maintain your daily devotional life. You can't point teens to the way unless you are in constant contact with the divine Guide. Spend much time in the secret closet of prayer.

5. Illustrate by others, not yourself. When you are preaching from the pulpit, or counseling in your study with teens, use the illustrations of others and do not refer to what you did when you were a boy. Never say, especially in counseling with teen-

agers on moral problems, "This is what Mrs. X and I did when we were your age."

6. Practice being practical. Don't be so heavenly-minded that you are no earthly good. Keep your counseling always on a spiritual level, but be practical in your sound advice.

7. Be yourself—there's only one of you. Don't mimic. The kids talk in their inner circles about a preacher who tries to be like someone else. They can spot a man who is not genuine. Today's teens admire an individualist because they feel that it takes time, study, and character to be different.

8. Don't look for pity, but expect to be kicked. Sympathy doesn't go with the modern age. You tell us from the pulpit that "Christ opened not His mouth" when He was ridiculed and disgraced for us. Therefore, don't expect to be pitied for any sacrifice you are making. Don't lower the dignity of your profession by expecting any kind of discount on respect. You will get your share of bumps. Take them like a man. That's what you preach, and the kids expect you to practice it.

9. Never be caught talking about anybody. Criticism is not supposed to be part of your character. Adopt the policy of never saying anything about anybody unless it's good.

10. Listen and be patient, remembering you were once young yourself. Don't get too busy and too irritated with a multitude of the same kinds of problems that come from teens. Look at those kids in the mirror of your own life when you were their age. Take a lot of time to listen to them; even if it takes hours and hours as they repeat their problems.

11. Be a man. Speak with authority. Don't always apologize for the things your parishioners don't do. Don't yell in the pulpit, but speak loudly and clearly enough that folks can hear and understand you. Your content might be the best, but if your voice is weak, the young people will pronounce you dead. A minister without boldness is like a smooth file, a knife without an edge, or a sentinel who is afraid to fire his gun. "If men will be bold in sin, ministers must be bold to reprove." Every minister of the gospel should address his audience with the zeal of a friend, the generous energy of a father, and with the exuberant affection of a mother.

12. Recommend and commend, but don't dictate. Young people turn a deaf ear and build up a stony heart against anybody who they feel is forcing them to do something. A dogmatic pastor is not well-received by the modern teenage crowds. The kids classify him as a square and talk about him as someone who thinks he is always right. However, if the young people feel that the pastor has taken time to investigate their personal need and has a concrete plan or suggestion, mingled with a confidence in young people, they respond very pleasantly. If you are known as a pastor who can be trusted and a pastor who appreciates what has been done and thus exercises the important tool of commendation, you are going to find young people hanging around you. A good minister of Jesus Christ is not a dictator. He must preach the divine Word, not human wisdom. He must preach Christ, not culture. He must preach regeneration, not reformation; and he must

preach Christian action, not smug satisfaction. Someone has wisely said that there are three essentials of good preaching: Stand up, speak up, and shut up! I would add one more: live up!

13. Don't be a deadpan. There are too many who have the idea that their dignity is wrapped up in their soberness. Look bright. A good salesman will never sell his product by trying to impress people with a long, sober face. Your clothing has a lot to do with the way young people receive you. Look neat, but show them that you are not so outdated that you always wear the cloak of the morgue. Then, I advise you to think bright. You can't always put your arm around an energetic teen and in tones which are draped with pessimism try to help him with his problem. Keep up-to-date. Think on those things which are spiritual and learn to apply them to each individual teen case. Then, by all means, act bright. The kids in our town catalogued all the preachers in the same group with a sad, stooped-shouldered fellow who wore baggy trousers. He always looked as though he had just lost his last friend.

Then, this closing instruction as to your preaching: I'm afraid too many preachers try to impress congregations with all the things they know. You and I would be surprised to find out how quickly teens catch on. You must be an interesting, lively preacher so that your dignity is mingled with enthusiasm. Jesus was an interesting preacher, and here, as in all other respects, He serves as a model for preachers today. Someone said of his preacher, "He can dive in deeper, stay under longer, and come up drier than anybody I have ever known." It is said in one congregation, after the pastor had delivered an hour-long sermon in a monotone that was interesting to him and no one else, the choir sang very appropriately, "We'll Understand It Better By and By." You can be the smartest man in your theology class, but if your young people cannot understand what you say, you are going to lose them fast.